Kites

Twelve Easy-to-Make High Fliers

Written by Norma Dixon

Illustrated by Linda Hendry

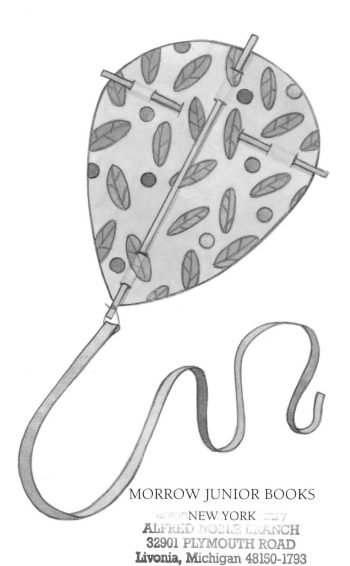

MORROW JUNIOR BOOKS

NEW YORK

NUV 0 6 1996

First published in Canada in 1995 by Kids Can Press,
29 Birch Avenue, Toronto, Ontario, Canada M4V 1E2

Printed in the United States of America.

1 2 3 4 5 6 7 8 9 10

Library of Congress Cataloging-in-Publication Data
Dixon, Norma.
Kites: twelve easy-to-make high fliers / written by Norma Dixon;
illustrated by Linda Hendry.
p. cm.
Summary: Provides instructions for making and flying all kinds of kites,
including serpent, six-sided, shooting star, and flexible kites.
ISBN 0-688-14489-6 (trade)—ISBN 0-688-14490-X (library)
1. Kites—Design and construction—Juvenile literature. [1. Kites.
2. Handicraft.] I. Hendry, Linda. II. Title. TL759.5.D57 1996
629.133'32—dc20 95-18386 CIP AC

Contents

Introduction

For centuries people have been making kites from all kinds of unusual things, such as leaves or fur. Today we can use materials the first kite makers never heard of, like plastic garbage bags or rip-stop nylon. You can make kites that fly well from all kinds of materials. Whether you gather the things you need from around your home or buy them at a store, remember the kite-making rule: tough and light make a better kite.

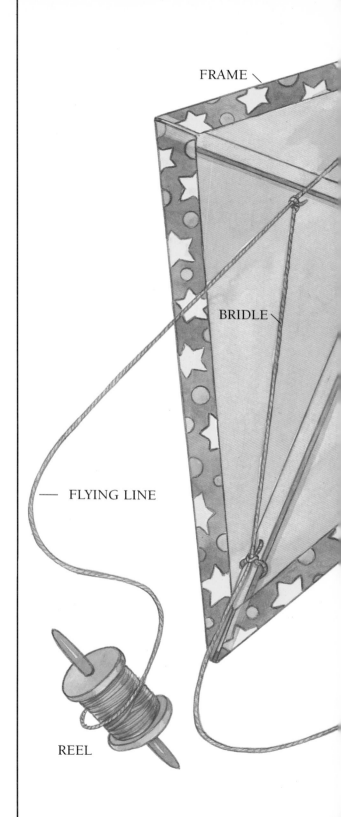

FRAME

BRIDLE

FLYING LINE

REEL

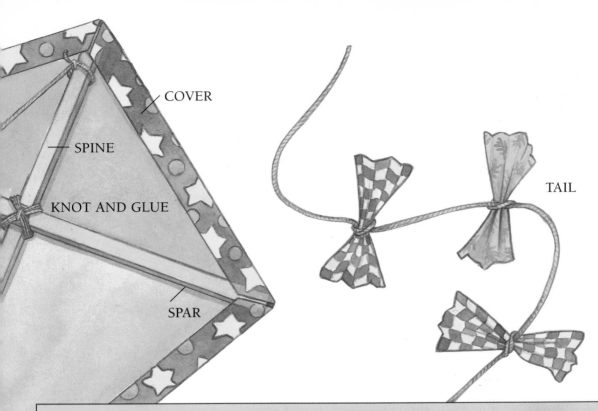

COVER

SPINE

KNOT AND GLUE

SPAR

TAIL

K I T E   P A R T S

SPINE   the up-and-down, or vertical, stick that you build your kite around

SPAR   the support stick or sticks placed crossways or at a slant over the spine. Sometimes spars are curved or bowed.

FRAME   the joined spine and spars, usually with a string connecting their ends, that form the shape of your kite and make a support for the cover

COVER   the paper, plastic or cloth that covers the frame to make a kite

BRIDLE   one or more strings attached to the spine or spars, which help control your kite in the air

FLYING LINE   the string running from the kite's bridle, which you hold to fly your kite

TAIL   the long strip of paper, plastic or ribbon that helps to keep your kite balanced in flight. Some kites don't need tails.

REEL   the gadget you use to wind your flying line, to keep it from getting tangled or running away

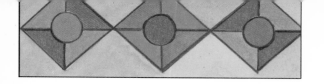

Materials and general instructions

To make a kite that really flies, it is important to use the right materials and to follow carefully some basic instructions.

The information on these pages will get you off the ground. You may want to refer back to them while you're making your kite.

TOOLS FOR KITE MAKERS

Always ask an adult for help with knives and saws.

KNIFE – for notching the ends of spines and spars

SAW – for cutting spines and spars

SCISSORS – strong and sharp enough to cut paper, plastic or fabric

TAPE – transparent tape for paper or plastic kites, or cloth tape for cloth kites

GLUE – good-quality, waterproof white glue for reinforcing knots and attaching the cover to the frame

BALL OF STRONG THREAD OR STRING – for lines and bridles, for binding spars to the spine and for framing

NEEDLES AND PINS – for threading on bridle strings or giving some kites a few stitches

COVERS

Newspaper, brown wrapping paper, tissue paper and crepe paper can all be used to make kite covers. When you use paper, reinforce the corners with tape — and don't get caught in a rainstorm!

Plastic garbage bags, grocery bags and lightweight plastic tarps make good waterproof kite covers. Cloth such as silk or rip-stop nylon is the kite-covering material that lasts longest.

For most kites you will need to cut your cover at least 2 cm (³/₄ inch) bigger than your frame all around. This will allow a margin of material to fold over the frame. After covering the frame, you can strengthen your cover with tape anywhere that it is folded over the end of a stick.

SPINES AND SPARS

Lightweight wood such as split bamboo, dowels and even twigs can be used for spines and spars. Make sure the sticks are an even thickness; otherwise, your kite may fly lopsided, or not at all.

Fiberglass rods are flexible, strong and light. You can buy these at hobby, hardware or kite-supply stores. Always have an adult saw or cut them for you. The invisible "sawdust" is dangerous to breathe and can cause a rash.

Cut a V-shaped notch 5 mm (¹/₄ inch) deep in each end of each stick. It's easier to cut the sticks if they're held in a vise or clamp. Ask an adult to help you with a knife or saw.

Glue the spars in place, or have someone hold them in place for you. Then secure them with crisscrossed string and cover the string with glue.

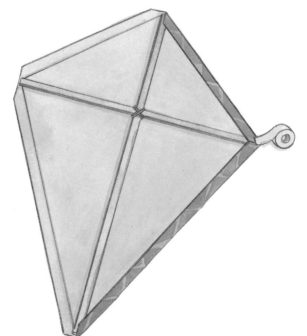

FRAMES, LINES AND BRIDLES

The heavy thread or light string used for stitching canvas or carpeting works well. Once again, the rule is light and strong for best results.

FRAME

To give your kite its frame, tie string to one end of a spar to anchor it and guide the string around all the notched spine and spar tips. Then untie the anchor knot, and tie both ends of the framing string together. Be sure the string is taut but not pulling.

BRIDLES

The bridle is a string about three times as long as your kite. For most kites, tie the bridle to both ends of the kite's spine, or tie it to opposite ends of a horizontal spar. Tie your flying line to the center of the bridle string. The bridle string on each side of the tie-on point is called a leg. Kites in this book that have three- or four-legged bridles have their own instructions.

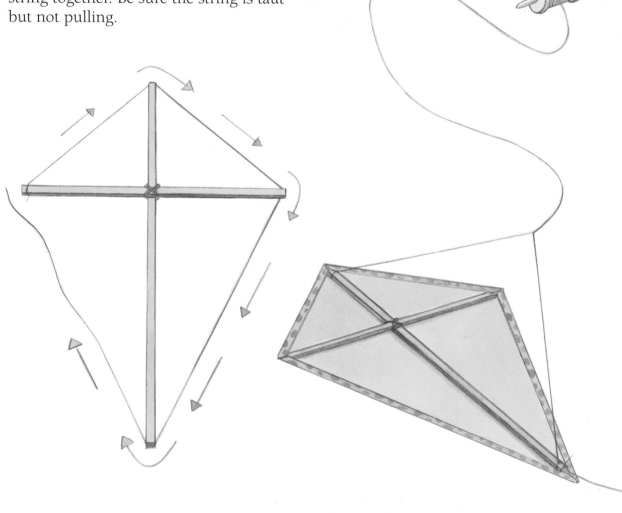

TAILS

Your kite tail should be a piece of string about $1\frac{1}{2}$ times the length of your kite's spine. Make bows for the tail by wrapping thread around the middle of small strips of crepe paper, ribbon, fabric pieces or other odds and ends. Tie the tail string around each finished bow; if you tie the bows to the tail, they'll slide down into a bunch at the end. Tie the tail securely to the bottom end of the spine.

You may have to experiment with the length of the tail, depending on how your kite flies.

TASSELS

Some kites have tassels for tails. You can make a tassel by stacking two or three ribbons or strips of paper about 60 cm (24 inches) long and 1 cm ($\frac{1}{2}$ inch) wide. Tie them together at the center. Tie them to the bottom of the spine or to the lowest tips of your kite's spars.

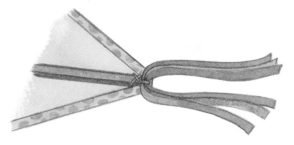

REELS

The simplest reel is a piece of wood or heavy cardboard with a notch cut in each end.

Try using an empty pop can. Make a hole in the top and bottom, and put a stick through. Tie your string to the stick, then wind it around the pop-can spool.

Avoid ball-shaped reels that will roll away easily if you drop them.

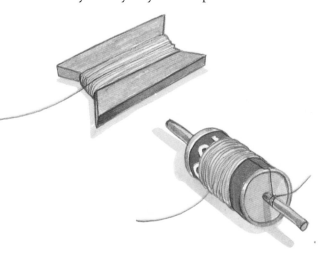

Decorating your kite

You can decorate your kite cover before you attach it to the frame, or wait until it's in place. You might want to test-fly your kite to make sure it flies well before adding too much decoration.

Kite designs that use two or three bold contrasting colors look best when your kite is in the air.

Waterproof felt markers are good for drawing designs on your kite because they won't smear if the kite lands on wet grass. Paints work well too.

Stamps or prints are a good way to make allover patterns.

Try gluing cutout designs to your kite to add color. Be careful that the cutouts don't add too much weight.

A few decorating ideas are shown here. You'll be able to think of lots more yourself.

OTHER FUN IDEAS

NOISEMAKER – Tie a piece of string to one end of a spine or spar. Pull it taut and tie it to another end. Fold a piece of paper lengthwise over the string and glue it in place. Cut the free edge into comblike teeth. When the wind catches the paper strips, you'll hear a rustling, whispering noise.

PAPER RACE – Have a race with a kite-flying friend. Cut a circle about the size of a saucer from a piece of paper. Cut a slit from the edge to the center of the circle. When your kite is flying, slide the paper circle over the kite line, as high up as you can reach. Jerk the kite string up and down until the wind catches the paper and pushes it up the string. See whose circle reaches the kite first.

NIGHT LIGHT – Try flying your kite after dark. Tape a mini-flashlight to your kite where the spine and lowest spar cross. Switch it on and let it fly. The kite disappears, and the flashlight becomes a mysterious light dancing in the sky. Be sure you know the area well when you're kite flying after dark so you don't bump into anything. Always take an adult with you.

Classic two-stick kite

When you think of kites, you usually think of this classic style first. It's a good kite to start with because it's one of the easiest to make.

YOU WILL NEED

spine, 95 cm (36 inches) long

spar, 85 cm (33 inches) long

knife

string

glue

paper, plastic or cloth for a cover

scissors

materials for making the tail

1 Cut a notch in each end of the sticks you are using for the spine and spar.

2 Place the short spar stick over the long spine stick about 25 cm (10 inches) down from the top of the spine. Crisscross string around the crossing point to hold it securely. Coat the string with glue.

3 Run a piece of string around all the notched tips of the sticks. Tie the ends together to form a frame. Make sure the string is taut.

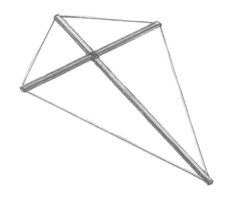

4 Place the frame on your cover material. Outline the kite shape, adding a margin 3 cm (1¼ inches) wide all around. Cut out the shape.

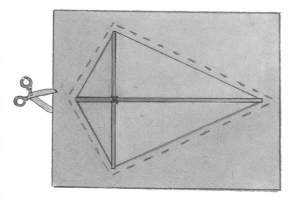

5 Trim the cover corners as shown. Fold the margins over the framing string.

6 Unfold the margins, spread on some glue, and press them over the string.

7 Attach a bridle string about 3 m (10 feet) long to the top and bottom of the spine. Tie your flying line about one-third of the way down your bridle string.

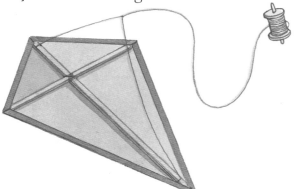

8 Make a tail 1½ times the length of the spine. For this kite, that would be about 140 cm (56 inches). See page 9 for tail-making tips.

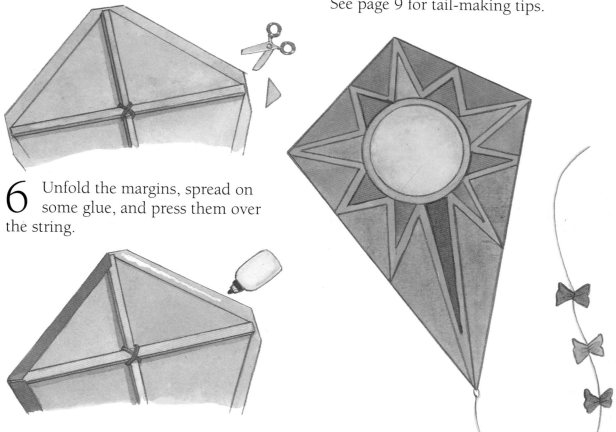

Mini-kite

This is one of the smallest kites you'll make. It is also called the Bermuda Children's Kite because originally it was a favorite of kids in Bermuda.

YOU WILL NEED

scrap paper
13 cm x 15 cm (5 x 6 inches)

brown wrapping paper,
gift-wrap paper or a paper bag
13 cm x 15 cm (5 x 6 inches)

scissors

ruler

2 thin sticks, one 13 cm (5 inches)
and one 15 cm (6 inches) long,
such as plastic swizzle sticks,
bamboo skewers or twigs

thread

a strip of crepe paper, tissue paper or
light ribbon about 2 m (6 feet) long
and 1.5 cm ($^1/_2$ inch) wide

1 Fold your scrap paper in half. Draw half the kite shape from the fold to the edge and back to the fold, just the way you would draw a heart shape, but without the dip in the top. Cut out your kite shape and open it up.

2 Trace the shape onto your final paper and cut it out.

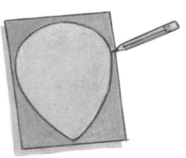

3 Punch ten holes with scissor tips (or a hole punch if you have one) in the paper as shown.

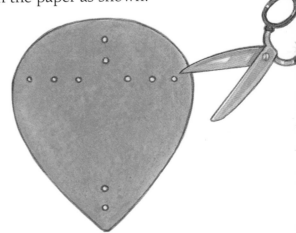

4 Carefully weave the two sticks in and out of the holes as shown.

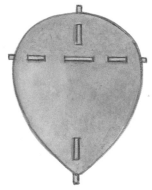

7 Tie another loop of thread to the bottom of the spine. Tape or tie your 2-m (6-foot) strip of paper or ribbon to the bottom for a tail.

5 Cut a piece of thread about 25 cm (10 inches) long for a bridle. Tie it to the spine.

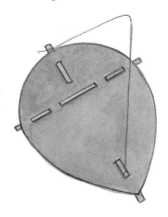

8 Tie your flying line to the thread loop on your bridle, and your kite is ready for takeoff.

6 Tie a small loop of thread to the bridle about 10 cm (3½ inches) from the top of the kite.

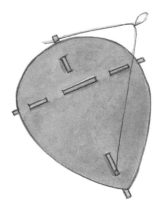

Serpent kite

First-time kite makers like this flying serpent because it not only looks great, it's also a snap to make. Color it scary!

YOU WILL NEED

spine, 50 cm (20 inches) long

2 spars, 35 cm (14 inches) long

knife

glue

string

brown wrapping paper

scissors

crepe paper

tape

paints or marker pens

1 Cut notches in the ends of your spine and spars. (See page 7.)

2 Tie and glue one spar to the base of the spine, and the other 10 cm (4 inches) down from the top of the spine.

3 Tie a string to one tip of the bottom spar. Guide this framing string around the other tips, and tie it to the other tip of the bottom spar.

4 Cut a sheet of brown wrapping paper 3 cm (1¼ inches) larger all around than the string outline. With the point of the paper at the top, draw the serpent's face.

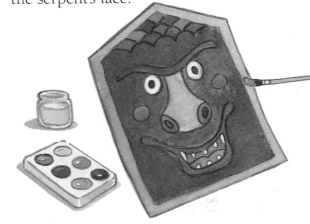

5 Trim the corners as shown. Spread glue on the 3-cm margins and fold them over the string. Snip the bottom margin to fit around the spine tip.

6 Make a tail from one long piece of crepe paper, about 8 m (26 feet) long. (If you have to glue two or three pieces of paper together, reinforce the glued seams with tape.)

7 Cut the tail so that it is 20 cm (8 inches) wide at the head and tapers gradually to a point at the end. Decorate it with scales and zigzags and then glue or tape it to the bottom of the kite.

8 Tie a bridle to the kite as shown. The bridle should be about 160 cm (63 inches) long.

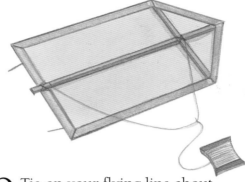

9 Tie on your flying line about one-third of the way down the bridle.

Six-sided kite

You can get this popular hexagonal kite ready for takeoff with just a little bit of work. Choose some brightly colored cover material.

YOU WILL NEED

3 spars, 70 cm (27 inches) long

knife

string

glue

paper or plastic cover material

scissors

streamers of narrow ribbon or paper

1 Cut a small notch in each end of three spars.

2 Cross the three spars and secure them with crisscrossed string. Adjust them so the tips are an even distance apart. Put glue on the string.

3 Run a framing string around the notches at the ends of the spars. Pull it taut. Tie the ends together.

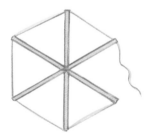

4 Place your frame on your cover material and trace around it, making it 3 cm (1¼ inches) larger all around. Cut out the shape.

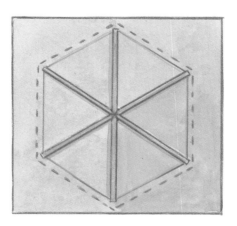

5 Trim the corners of the kite cover as shown. Fold the margins over the framing string and glue them down.

8 Tie streamer tails to the bottom of the kite.

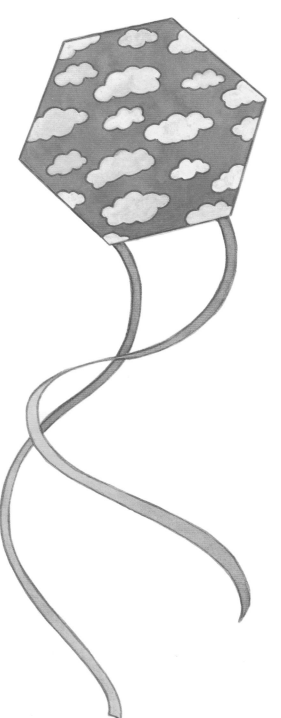

6 Cut one bridle string 105 cm (40 inches) long and tie it to the center of the kite. Cut two more bridle strings, each about 35 cm (14 inches) long, and tie them to the top of the kite.

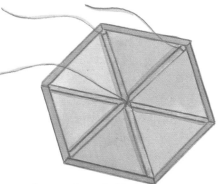

7 Knot the ends of all three strings together. Attach your flying line at that point.

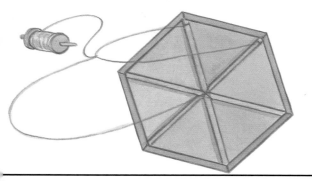

Flying fish

You can fly this fish like a kite, or tie it to a stick and use it for a wind sock.

1 Draw a fish shape at least 95 cm (36 inches) long on a big piece of paper. Give your fish a large, open mouth. Cut out your fish.

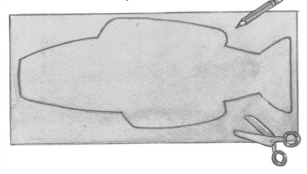

2 Trace the fish shape onto another piece of paper, and cut out this fish too. Decorate your fish.

3 Spread glue along the top and bottom edges of the back of each fish. Don't put glue on the mouth or tail because they have to be open to let the wind blow through. Glue the two fish together.

4 Open the mouth so it forms a circle. Bend a piece of wire into a circle the same size as the mouth.

5 Push the wire circle into the mouth and tape it in place.

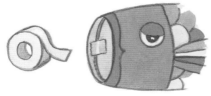

6 Make a hole on each side of the mouth, and reinforce it with a loose-leaf-paper reinforcement, or circles you cut from tape.

7 Tie a bridle string, about 50 cm (20 inches) long, through the holes.

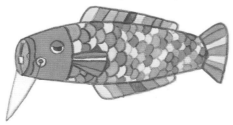

8 To fly your fish as a kite, tie a flying line at the midpoint of the bridle.

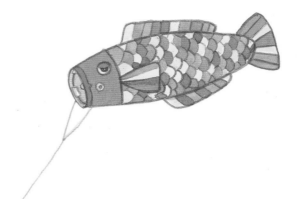

9 To make a wind sock for your yard or balcony, tie a piece of string about 20 cm (8 inches) long to the bridle, then tie the string to a pole.

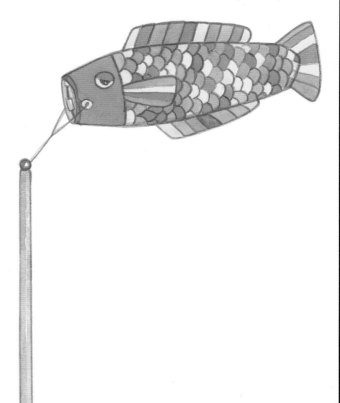

South American bird

This kite is a great flier. Just what you'd expect from a bird! Try decorating it with a feather pattern.

YOU WILL NEED

spine, 55 cm (22 inches) long

spar, 130 cm (50 inches) long

knife

string

newspaper or scrap paper

scissors

cloth

straight pins

needle and thread

1 Make a notch in the spine and spar at both ends. With crisscrossed string and glue, join the spar to the spine 15 cm (6 inches) down from the top of the spine.

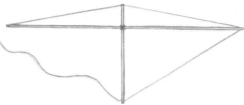

2 Tie string to the tip of a spar, and run it around the notched ends of the sticks. Tie the string ends together.

3 Place your frame on the scrap paper. Draw a bird shape with wingtips that touch each end of the spar. Draw the bird's head at the top of the spine. Draw the tail at the other end of the spine.

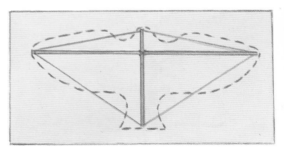

4 Draw a square tab about 3 cm (1¼ inches) long at each wingtip. Draw another square tab at the top of the head, and a fourth tab at the tail.

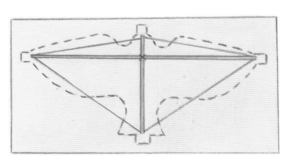

5 Cut out your paper pattern. Remember to cut around the tabs too.

6 Pin your paper pattern to your cloth cover and cut the shape out.

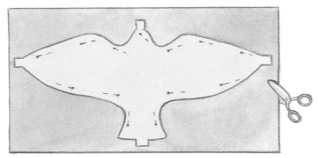

7 Place the frame on your cover. Fold over the tabs at the wingtips, head and tail, and pin the sides of each tab to form a pocket for a spine or spar end.

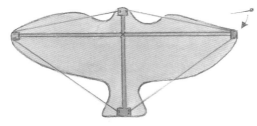

8 Sew only the sides of each pocket. The pockets on this kite are the only places where the cover is attached to the frame.

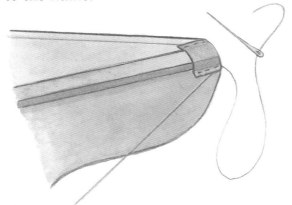

9 To make a four-legged bridle, cut a string 136 cm (54 inches) long. Cut the string in half. Tie one end of each string to the spar, each about halfway between one wingtip and the spine.

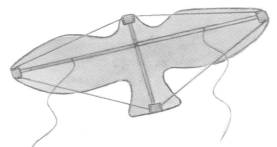

10 Cut another string 136 cm (54 inches) long. From this string, cut off a piece 63 cm (25 inches) long. Sew this string to the top of the head pocket. Sew the leftover piece of string to the tip of the tail pocket.

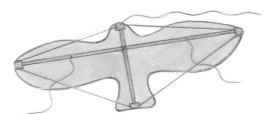

11 Tie the ends of all four strings together. Tie your flying line where the strings meet.

Flexible kite

The shape of this kite is formed by strings, and it looks something like a parachute.

1   Stick 2.5-cm (1-inch) pieces of tape on the plastic at the places marked 1, 2, 3 and 4. If your plastic is very thin, stick tape to both sides.

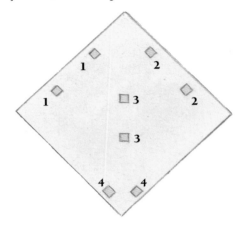

2   Cut three strings, each 30 cm (12 inches) long.

3   Thread your needle with one of the strings. Push the needle and string through one of the squares marked 1 to the other side of the plastic and back. Tie the end to the string. Sew the other end of the string through the other square 1 the same way and knot it.

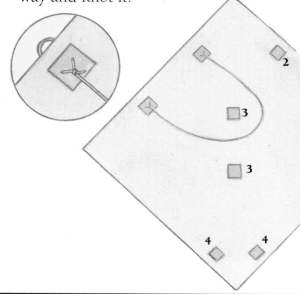

4 Thread the second string through points 2 the same way, and the third string through points 3. You will now have three loops of string.

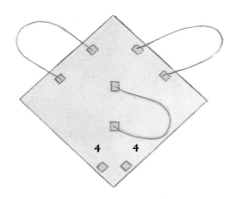

5 Cut a 15-cm (6-inch) string. Thread it through the two holes marked 4 to form a loop. Knot the ends. Tie the streamer tail to the center of the loop.

6 Tie your first three loops together at the center of each loop. Tie your flying line where they join.

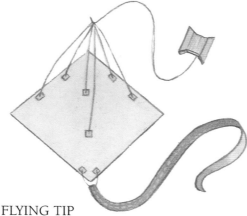

FLYING TIP
To launch this kite, hold it by the bridle until it catches the wind, then give it 1 to 2 m (3 to 6 feet) of line. As it lifts, gradually give it more line.

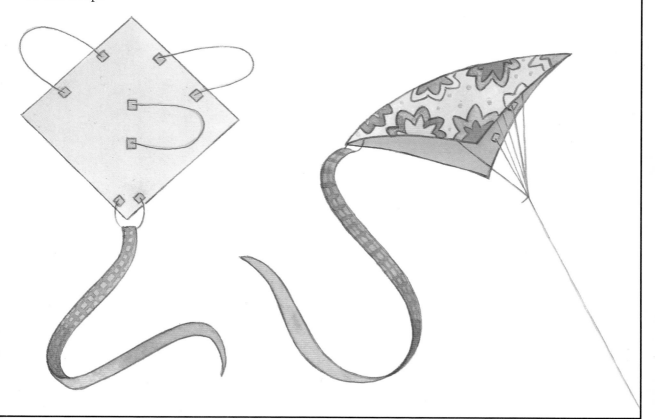

Scott sled kite

Kites have been around for thousands of years. This kite was invented in the 1950s, which makes it one of the newer styles. Get yours ready for the next breezy day.

YOU WILL NEED

sheet of plastic, 1 m wide and 90 cm high (39 x 35 inches), such as a garbage bag

scissors

2 spines, 90 cm (35 inches) long

tape

needle

string

1 Cut off the top corners of the plastic rectangle 25 cm (10 inches) in, and 25 cm (10 inches) down. Cut off the long bottom corners 25 cm (10 inches) in as well.

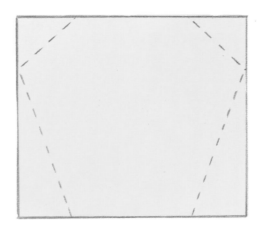

2 Cut a triangular hole about 15 cm (6 inches) up from the bottom, in the middle of the plastic. Make the bottom edge of the triangle 20 cm (8½ inches).

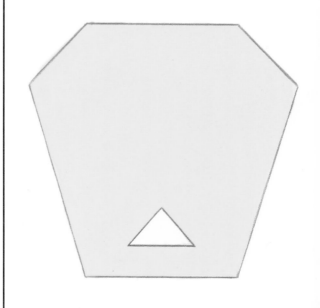

3 Tape the spines to the plastic in the positions shown.

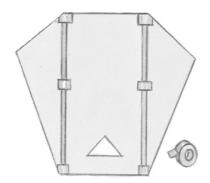

4 Cut two 3-cm (1¼-inch) squares of tape and stick them to the two outside corners as shown. These will reinforce the corners where you attach the bridle.

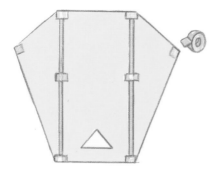

5 Cut a bridle string 1.5 m (5 feet) long. Thread the string through your needle and pull an end through each reinforced corner. Knot each end.

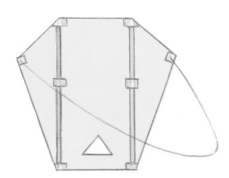

6 Tie your flying line to the center of the bridle.

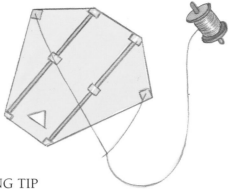

FLYING TIP

The Scott sled flies well once it is in the air, but sometimes it can be tricky to launch. Feed out your flying line slowly. If you let it out too fast, the sled might fold up. Be sure your bridle is the right length — 1.5 m (5 feet). If it is shorter or longer, the kite might fall.

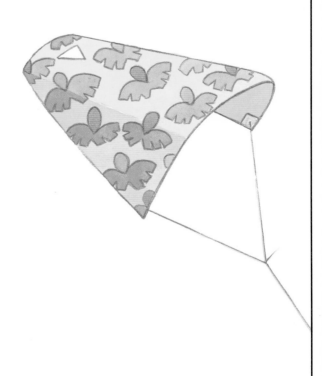

27

Shooting star

Make this star performer stand out by choosing bright or neon colors for the cover.

YOU WILL NEED

spine, 1 m (39 inches) long

2 spars, 85 cm (33 inches) long

knife

string

glue

scissors

cover material, 103 cm x 90 cm (40 x 34 inches)

tape

needle and strong thread

streamers, ribbon, crepe paper or foil

1 Cut notches in the ends of the spine and spars.

2 Tie and glue the sticks together as shown, with the two spars 25 cm (10 inches) from the ends of the spine.

3 Tie string to one end of a spar and run it around the notched end of the spine that is farthest away. Bring the string back to the opposite end of the spar to form a triangle.

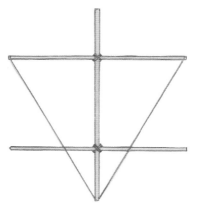

4 Tie the string to the spar. Cut off any leftover string about 1 cm (¹/₂ inch) from your knot.

5 Tie a second string triangle using the other spar.

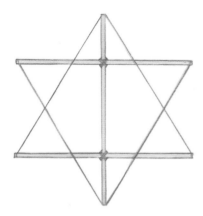

6 Place the star frame on your cover material and trace it, making it 3 cm (1¼ inches) larger all around.

7 Trim the corners as shown. Fold the 3-cm margin over the strings.

8 Glue down the margins. Strengthen each corner with a triangle of tape.

9 Tie a bridle to the frame as shown. The bridle string should be about 3 m (10 feet) long. Tie your flying line to the center of the bridle.

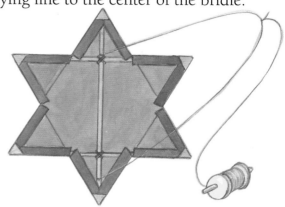

10 Attach three streamers to the lowest three points on the star with a needle and strong thread. Try to pierce your cover only twice at each reinforced corner. Add tinsel or foil strips to your streamer tails, if you like.

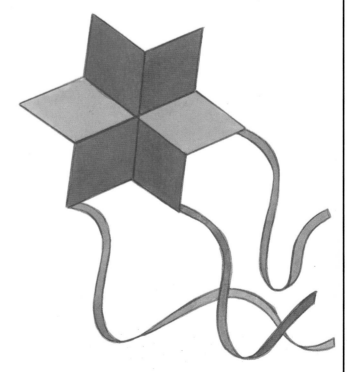

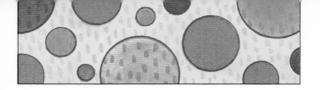

Caterpillar kite

This creepy-crawler kite might take a little longer to make than some other kites, but the steps are simple. You can turn it into a centipede or a dragon.

YOU WILL NEED

8 pieces of flexible but shape-holding material, 100 cm (40 inches) long, such as split bamboo, willow strips or wire

16 spars, 38 cm (15 inches) long

cover material

heavy-duty tape

scissors

string

glue

wire cutters (if you're using wire)

material for streamers (optional)

1 Carefully bend one stick or wire into a ring. Overlap the ends 2 cm (³/₄ inch) and tape them together firmly. You might want to have someone hold the ring while you tape it, so it doesn't spring open.

2 Tie two spars together in the center to form a cross.

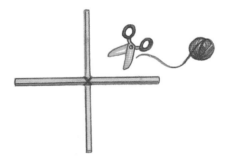

3 Place the cross on the ring so each tip extends an even distance over the edge. Tie the cross to the ring at all four crossing places and coat the knots with glue.

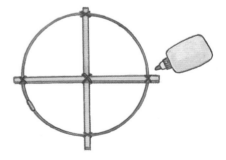

4 Use the same method to make seven more circular frames.

5 Place a frame on the cover material and trace around it, allowing a margin of 3 cm (1¼ inches). You will need to make eight circular covers.

6 Notch the edges of each of the covers so they will fit neatly. Fold each cover over a frame, allowing the spar tips to stick out. Glue down the margin.

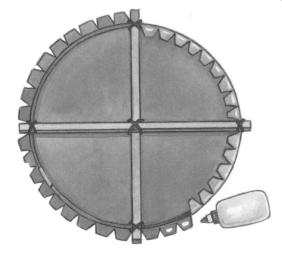

7 Decorate the covered ring that will fly at the front of your kite with a face, if you like.

8 Join the covered rings together by tying string from the spar tips of each covered ring to the spar tips of the next covered ring. Keep the distance between the rings 25 cm (10 inches).

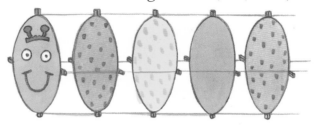

9 Make a bridle with three legs. Tie a 38-cm (15-inch) leg to each spar on each side of the head. Tie a 33-cm (13-inch) leg to the spar at the top of the head. Tie the ends of the three bridle lines together. Tie your flying line to the place where the bridle lines are knotted.

DECORATING TIPS
• Try using a different-colored cover for each frame.
• Turn your caterpillar into a centipede with streamer legs.
• Make a fierce-faced dragon with head and tail streamers.

Box kite

The earliest airplanes were modeled after box kites. These kites also have been used in scientific experiments, and people have even tried to fly with them!

YOU WILL NEED

4 spines, 0.5 cm x 1 cm x 100 cm
($^1/_4$ x $^3/_8$ x 40 inches)

4 spars, 0.5 cm x 1.25 cm x 43 cm
($^1/_4$ x $^1/_2$ x 17 inches)

2 sheets of cover material, each 30 cm
x 125 cm (12 x 49 inches)

knife

glue

string

scissors

tape

ruler

small plastic ring

1 Lay the two sheets of cover material side by side, with the inside facing up. Measure and mark each sheet into four 30-cm (12-inch) sections. There will be a 5-cm (1-inch) flap at the end of each sheet.

2 Adjust the two sheets of cover material so that the outer edges are 1 m (40 inches) apart, with all the ruled marks aligned.

3 Glue the narrow edge of a spine along the line closest to the 5-cm (1-inch) flaps. Place it on the side of the line closest to the flaps.

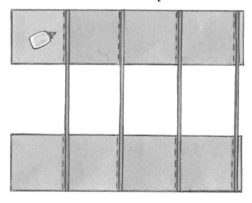

4 Glue the remaining spines, narrow edge down, along the other lines. Keep all the spines on the same side of the lines. Keep the outside distance of the covers at 1 m (40 inches). Let the glue dry.

5 Spread glue on the outside of each 5-cm (1-inch) flap. Press the free edge of a 30-cm (12-inch) cover section over each glued flap to line up neatly with the edges of the covered spines.

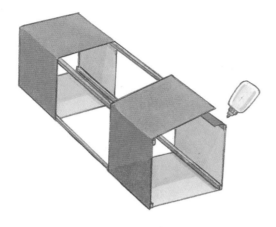

6 In the end of each spar, make a notch that is 0.5 cm ($^1/_4$ inch) wide and 1 cm ($^3/_8$ inch) deep. Each spar should measure 41 cm (16 $^1/_8$ inches) from notch to notch.

7 Trim the corners of each spar as shown.

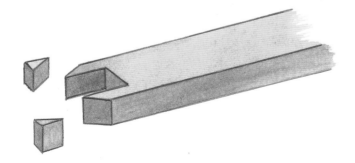

8 Form the box shape by inserting the spars crossed in pairs, with the notched ends fitted over the spines, about midpoint on the covers. You may have to shorten the spar length for a snug fit. If you do shorten your crossed spars, keep each pair the same length between notches.

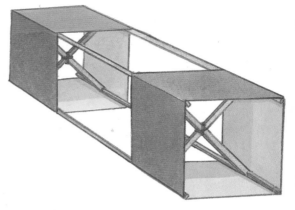

9 When the crossed spars are fitted, tie each pair together.

10 Pierce bridle string holes in the cover on both sides of two spines at points 1 and 2. Tie 63-cm (25-inch) bridle strings to the upper end at 1. Tie 75-cm (30-inch) bridle strings to the lower end at 2. Tie all four ends to a plastic ring. Tie your flying line to the ring.

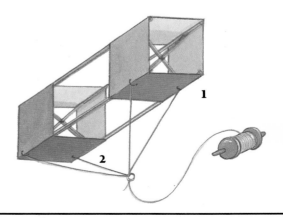

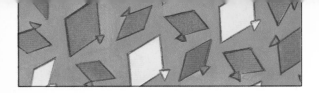

Fighter kite

A fighter-kite buff named Al Berman developed this version of the more complicated true fighter kite. This simplified model is easy to make and even easier to fly.

1 On a piece of scrap paper, draw a line 70 cm (28 inches) long. Draw a 44-cm (16$^{1}/_{4}$-inch) line crossing it in the center. Join the tips of the lines to form a diamond with equal sides. Cut out the diamond and use it as a pattern to cut your cover.

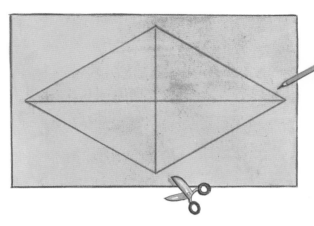

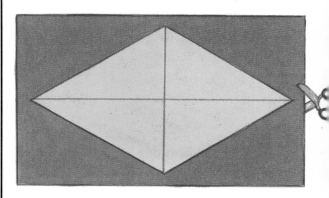

2 Cut a triangle that's 16 cm (6$^{1}/_{2}$ inches) wide at the base and 8 cm (3$^{1}/_{4}$ inches) high from your cover material. This will be a stabilizer, which is used instead of a tail on fighter kites.

3 Glue the stabilizer triangle to the front of the cover, with the long side 4 cm (1⅝ inches) from the bottom tip of the cover.

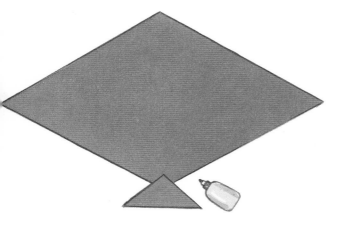

4 Reinforce the edges of the cover, on the back side, with long strips of tape.

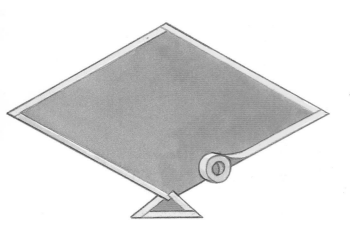

5 Stick a piece of heavy-duty tape about 8 cm (3 inches) from the nose of the kite, where the spine and spar will cross. Stick another piece 14 cm (5½ inches) from the bottom edge of the kite. These will be reinforcements for bridle strings.

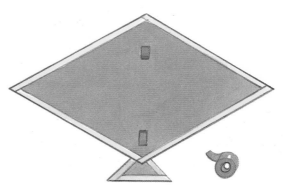

6 Spread glue on the spine. Place it in the center of the cover with both ends extending about 0.5 cm (³⁄₁₆ inch) over the ends. Press down, and let the glue dry.

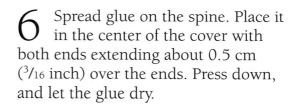

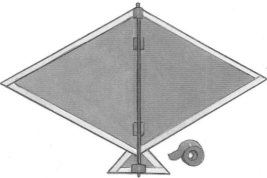

7 Secure the spine to the cover at the nose end and the tail end with heavy-duty tape.

8 Soak the spar dowel in hot water for about ten minutes or until it bends easily.

9 Bend the soaked spar into a curve that is 70 cm (28 inches) from tip to tip. The two ends of the curve should meet the two tips of the cover that are 70 cm (28 inches) apart.

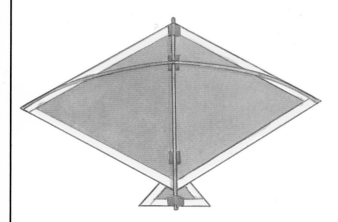

10 Center the curved spar on the spine with the tips touching the tips of the cover. Attach it with four pieces of heavy-duty tape in the positions shown.

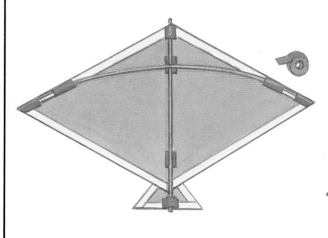

11 Glue the 10-cm (4-inch) bamboo slivers to the back edges of the stabilizer.

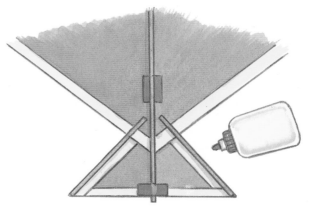

12 Make a hole in the tape and thread a bridle string through the tape at 1. Tie it around the cross of the spine and bow. Thread another bridle string through the tape at 2 and tie it to the spine. Knot the free ends of the string to a small plastic ring. The top bridle leg should be 33 cm (13 inches) from cover to ring. The bottom leg should be 38 cm (15 inches) from cover to ring. Tie your flying line to the ring.

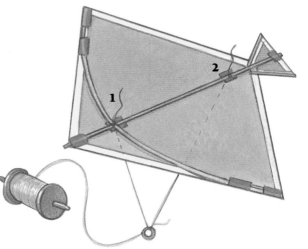

FLYING YOUR FIGHTER KITE

The fighter is a fast-moving and lively kite because it was originally designed for contests where fighter kites attack each other to cut flying lines. With a little practice, you'll be able to make your fighter kite dance and twist at your command. Check page 38 for directions on launching your kite, and then follow these tips for flying your fighter.

• Don't let out too much flying line. The higher a fighter goes, the less control you have over it. The fighter is correctly airborne when it keeps its position with little slack and you can feel it at the end of your line.

• To make your fighter kite zigzag, give short tugs to the flying line.

• To change the flying direction, slowly let out line. This will cause the kite to relax and float or to spin around. When the nose is pointing in the direction you want, pull on the line, and the kite will follow in that direction.

• To make a fighter kite start a nosedive, quickly pull in on the line. Stop the dive by quickly letting out line.

• Use smooth hand-over-hand motions to adjust your fighter kite's position. The best way to control your fighter is to stand with your elbows close to your side and your hands in front of your chest. Always use two hands on the line.

• If you think your fighter kite is going to crash, let out line. Don't pull in the line. This will make the kite fly faster and crash harder.

• Don't run with your fighter kite. Running causes erratic flight patterns that could make it crash.

Launching
your kite

1. Stand with your back to the wind and unwind about 5 m (16 feet) of line.

2. Hold the kite by its lowest corner. If it has a tail, trail the tail away from you.

3. If there is a steady breeze, toss the kite upward, and take a few steps backward.

4. As the kite starts to rise, gradually let out the string you have already unwound.

5. Keep the string taut. Give it short tugs to get the kite higher.

6. If there's not much wind, run a short distance to get your kite airborne.

7. If the wind is strong and your kite still won't take off, try adjusting the length of the bridle or tail.

ONCE IT'S FLYING

Feed out line slowly. Make sure the slack is taken up each time before you let out more line or your kite could lose height.

If your kite line tangles with someone else's, walk toward each other. The kites can be separated by exchanging reels, or walking around each other.

You'll want to watch your kite once it's flying, but remember to check where you're going too!

LANDING YOUR KITE

If the breeze is light, reel in the line while walking toward your kite. When the kite is about 15 m (50 feet) away, let the line go slack. The kite will flutter to the ground.

If the breeze is strong, you can reel the kite right down to your hand so that it never touches the ground.

If your kite falls to the ground, walk to it. Pulling the kite to you by the string could break it.

KITE-FLYING WEATHER

A light steady breeze is best for kite flying. Blustery days can make your kite hard to control.

Don't fly your kite on extremely windy days or it will be blown away or torn to pieces.

You'll often find perfect kite-flying conditions at the seaside, or in open areas beside large bodies of water.

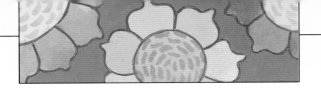

Safety rules
for kite
fliers

If a storm comes up, bring your kite down immediately. Don't launch your kite at all if it's a stormy day.

Keep away from power lines. If your kite gets tangled in a power line, call the utility company. Don't try to get it down yourself.

Never fly near a busy street or railway tracks.

Never use metal for any part of your kite or line.

Before you launch your kite, look around the area where you will be flying it. Make sure there's nothing to trip on or bump into.

Don't fly near crowds of people. If your kite falls, the string could trip people.

Don't fly too close to trees or your kite could become entangled or torn.

Wear gloves, especially on very windy days. A kite that is pulling hard can cause string cuts.

Have fun kite flying in a hazard-free open place such as a beach, playing field, park or meadow.